cardamom and lime

cardamom and lime

Recipes from the Arabian Gulf

SARAH AL-HAMAD

INTERLINK BOOKS

An imprint of Interlink Publishing Group, Inc.

For baba

First published in paperback in 2011 by
Interlink Books
An imprint of Interlink Publishing Group, Inc.
46 Crosby Street, Northampton, Massachusetts, 01060
www.interlinkbooks.com

ISBN 978-1-56656-849-4

Editor: Clare Sayer
Americanization: Lynne Saner
Food Consultant: Hiltrud Schulz
Recipe photographs: Sue Atkinson
Location photography: Sarah al-Hamad
Food stylist: Sunil Vijayakar
Stylist: Roisin Nield
Design: bluegumdesigners.com
Editorial Direction: Rosemary Wilkinson
Production: Hazel Kirkman

Reproduction by Pica Digital PTE Ltd, Singapore
Printed and bound in Singapore by Tien Wah Press PTE Ltd

To request our 40-page full-color catalog,
please call us toll free at **1-800-238-LINK**,
visit our website at **www.interlinkbooks.com**,
or send us an email: **info@interlinkbooks.com**

Contents

introduction

THE ARABIAN GULF consists of Bahrain, Oman, Kuwait, Qatar, the United Arab Emirates, and Saudi Arabia: a cluster of countries dotting the Arabian Sea coast that collectively are called al-Khaleej. This is a book about the food of the Arabian Gulf.

For hundreds of years the deserts and ports of the Arabian peninsula were inhabited by disparate tribes. Originally, the bedouin roaming the deserts relied heavily on a diet of dates and dairy products, rarely meat. Life was difficult and there were few natural resources.

In the pre-oil days, the Gulf's main sources of livelihood were pearling and trade. Later the merchants' travels brought a wide array of imported food items and methods of cooking. Arabia has long been a center of trade. Its position on the trade route from Africa to India was fortuitous, and it was on the *dhows* (traditional Arab sailing vessels) from India that the first spices and ingredients entered the region. Fragrant cardamom pods, cloves, saffron threads, cumin seeds, chili, and curry powder – and long-grain basmati rice. The food of the Gulf is largely a combination of Indian, Persian, and Turkish cuisine.

Cultures living by the sea (*al-bahar*) inevitably develop a closeness to it. Wherever you go in the Gulf – most khaleeji cities are built up along their coastlines – the sea is ever-present and a source of beauty. One of my favorite films is the Kuwaiti *Bas ya bahar* (1971), a sensitive yet cheerless rendering of life in the days when pearling was the common man's fate. The film beautifully illustrates this give and take with the sea and its dominance in everyday affairs. Pearling is obsolete today but the sea remains a strong symbol of the past. It is still vital to the economies of the area. Sea-sports and fishing are also popular.

The Gulf went from relative poverty to astonishing prosperity in the span of half a century. It now has one of the highest birth rates in the world. Seen as a land of opportunity, the region started attracting South Asians in the 1960s. This phenomenon affected people's dietary habits. While researching this book, most of the cooks I met were from India or Bangladesh. These migrant workers may live and work for decades in the Gulf, integrating into the families they join. A cook's training involves

learning traditional recipes as well as continental dishes like pasta, fancy salads, and desserts. A source of pride and envy, cooks are regularly "loaned out" to friends to teach other cooks a special dish or train newcomers. It is common for households to have a cook, even if the homemaker is a good one herself. Families are large and food sharing is central to local life.

To understand food-sharing is to get at the core of the role food plays in mediating social relations in the Gulf. In the olden

days, communities were small. Neighborhoods consisted of houses clustered together and socializing took place mostly among men in an open courtyard where they gathered and strangers were easily identified. A woman's place was firmly in the home, her social affairs confined to relatives and neighbors. Homemaking and childrearing would have been her primary roles. The housewife would cook every day, always making a little extra to share with neighbors or surprise guests.

In much the same way nowadays, lunch or dinner is offered at happy occasions but also at times of bereavement. Relatives and neighbors still engage in food exchanges that can last for years, with dishes traveling between homes. Wealthier households with large social networks have a quasi-dedicated catering system complete with hotel-style stainless steel boxes and transport van.

Food also tops the list of gifts to bring back from trips abroad. I remember crates of Alfonso mangos appearing every year at the same time, beautifully ripe and sweet, sent from India by one of my father's friends, or sacks of pistachios brought back from Iran, honey from Yemen, wonderful sesame-covered biscuits from Syria and Lebanon, and dates sent over from Saudi Arabia – each country renowned for a special food.

A venue where food makes a strong appearance is the *diwan* or *diwaniyya* (also known as the *majlis* in some countries), that most important of informal social institutions. The diwaniyya is typically a male social space where friends and relatives gather, usually in the evenings, to catch up, talk business or politics, or to gossip. It can be a simple room attached to a person's house, or a lavish hall where weddings and other rites are held. Diwaniyyas are family-specific. In Kuwait, the institution is especially strong and most local families will have one – it is a mark of status and prestige. Tea, coffee, and fresh juices are a fixture at these gatherings, finger foods like *sambousa* (samosas) and *batata chab* (potato "chops") are sometimes offered and dinner is served when the gathering thins out to family members.

No dish typifies Gulf cuisine better than the *machbous*. Inspired by the magnificent Persian and Indian biryanis, the machbous derives its name from the Arabic for compressed, *kabs*. It is a cooking method which reuses the spiced water used to cook meat or fish to suffuse the rice, marrying the ingredients and spices together. The resulting dish is a celebration of robust perfumes and ingredients, scented with cardamom, cloves, and cinnamon. There are many types of machbous (pl. *michabees*) – lamb, chicken, shrimp, and fish machbous are weekly menu fixtures, while truffle machbous and duck machbous are seasonal delicacies. Once learned, machbous-making can be adapted to include a variety of ingredients.

The Arabic for rice is *riz/ruz*, but in the Gulf it is *'aish* – or Living – evidence of its elevated status. Here lunch is the main meal of the day. Because of the heat, the working day starts early, usually around 7am, and ends at about 2pm. People lunch late and heartily and dinner is a meager affair by comparison. In our home and wherever I have lunched over the years, it is inconceivable that lunch be served without rice. The same applies to nearly every household in the Gulf. Rice is bought by the sackful.

Rice may be the unrivaled staple food today but it wasn't always so. Before trade introduced it to the peoples of the coast, and at times of scarcity, locally farmed grains like barley, *jareesh* (coarse wheat), and lentils were used. These would be cooked with whatever vegetables were in season (rarer still with meat) for several hours, then beaten to a savory porridge that was nutritious and filling. Wholesome grain-based dishes are still very popular, especially at Ramadhan and in winter.

Combining sweet and savory is also characteristic of Gulf cuisine. Raisins and crispy onions are sprinkled over rice and savory porridges, fish is served with date-sweetened rice, eggs accompany some puddings and desserts. Eating dates throughout the meal, in between morsels of machbous or rice, is common. Bowls of dates always accompany the main meal.

The most important regional food – and my great weakness – is the date fruit, *tamr*. Its value as a cultural player transcends its significant culinary worth. As a child I would hear my father say that a man could live on dates and yogurt alone, so complete and nutritious is the combination. Date palms are highly prized, their ownership a source of pride and prestige. I have never seen an unkempt, neglected palm tree – the mere idea seems subversive, even unreligious (date palms are the most frequently

mentioned fruit-bearing tree in the *Quran*). Each year the palms are pollinated and pruned. Only female trees bear fruit (the male ones pollinate), their fruits patiently awaited. The yield is stored for eating and cooking and any extra divided up among family and friends. The best known kinds are the *khlass* and the *birhi*, but there are myriad varieties, each with a distinctive shape, sweetness, texture, and color. Most of the dessert dishes in this book are made with dates, their high-energy, nourishing flesh perfectly suited to the region's arid, austere climate. In addition to its valuable fruit, the palm's juice (*dibs*) is used for baking and cooking and its branches for weaving baskets and mats.

Another important local produce is the dried lime, *lumi*, widely used to add sourness to stews and soups. Originally from Oman, but also popular in Persian cooking, lumi and dates are the two locally cultivated ingredients.

Perhaps because alcohol is forbidden and mostly avoided in the Gulf, food is *Big*. It occupies a central position in local life and culture. It is a means of communication and a social marker, a peace-offering, a way of demonstrating largesse and hospitality to friends and family, a form of one-upmanship, a conversation starter, a boredom buster, and an arena for female competitiveness. Recipes are coveted and secretly exchanged. Specialities are shown off at gatherings – cooking and eating are a big part of life.

What astounds is the sheer expanse of the food industry, in evidence everywhere – the heaving, crumbling old souks rubbing shoulders with gleaming megamarkets, price-controlled local co-operatives and neighborhood corner shops; fast food giants like McDonald's and Pizza Hut wooing customers with scintillating highway billboards; smaller, Middle-Eastern *shawarma* and *kushari* kiosks and the speciality restaurants catering to migrant workers from the Philippines, India, and Egypt; the sweet factories, flour mills, fruit and vegetable wholesalers, livestock importers, date merchants, fish markets, spice shops, and the plethora of stylish, high-end, world-food restaurants.

When I embarked on this project, I had no idea what treasures awaited me. Not only how much fun I would have recording these recipes, photographing street food and souks and cooks at work, and savoring the results, but the people I would meet: fishermen fresh off the dhows, effervescent housewives, Indian and Bangladeshi cooks, and pastry chefs fluent in *Khaleeji* Arabic, tea-sipping grocers, butchers, caterers, shawarma carvers, date and spice merchants, bakers, and legions of eaters.

The bulk of these recipes I collected from family and friends and friends of family and friends of friends. One cook led me to another, and wherever I went there was great generosity in discussions about food and sharing of culinary tidbits and recipes. I didn't encounter any ambivalence about food. Overwhelmingly, I found food associated with good things – pleasure, companionship, and tradition. In conceiving this book, my intention had been to introduce the Arabian Gulf through its cuisine and the diverse culinary traditions that have shaped it; I also wanted to preserve, in words and images, the "traditional" markets and foods of the Gulf vis-à-vis an encroaching fast food culture.

The recipes in this book were recorded while each dish was being cooked. My camera transformed kitchens into studios and cooks into chefs and at the end of every day we all gathered around my laptop screen. Months later and thousands of miles away, the images would jog my memory when gaps appeared in the notes. Once the recipes were on paper I tested them on eager friends. That was fun, and enabled me to understand the characteristic nature of Gulf cuisine, how varied and individual

it is, and that the proof is in the spicing – how much is used and which spices with which foods is where the difference lies. There are as many ways of spicing a dal soup as there are dal recipes (and there are a few!). Invariably, the distinction lies with the cooks, their culinary background, and each household's preferences. The recipes were somewhat modified to suit my taste; you should adapt them to yours. The quantities of spices used are guidelines only. Gulf cuisine is rarely available at restaurants (I know of only two in the world) because every household has a set of signature dishes and its own way of making flavorsome food. I have tried to collect the recipes most common to all six Gulf countries. But no region is monolithic and cultural differences are what add spice to life.

rice

mashkhoul

FRAGRANT WHITE RICE

IF THERE IS one dish to master in the Gulf it is *mashkhoul* – or *'aish*, as the locals call it – the starting point for all cooking and eating. I've watched rice being cooked hundreds of times – the grains are washed and rinsed carefully, they change color and swell as they cook and finally release a glorious aroma during steaming. Cooking rice is a comforting, familiar ritual. This is probably why a bowl of aromatic, fluffy rice topped with crispy onions is considered pure bliss.

1 lb 2 oz basmati rice
1 lemon wedge
1 tbsp vegetable oil
2 cardamom pods
1 cinnamon stick
salt to taste

FOR THE HAKOUKA
pinch of saffron strands
3 tbsp vegetable oil
1 onion, finely chopped

FOR THE FURQA'
5 tbsp vegetable oil
2 onions, thinly sliced

serves 4

Wash the rice and leave to soak for 30 minutes. Rinse until the water runs clear, then drain.

Soak the saffron strands for the hakouka in 3–4 tablespoons of warm water for at least 30 minutes.

Bring a large pan of salted water to a boil and add the lemon, vegetable oil, cardamom, cinnamon, and salt. Pour in the rice and bring to a boil, cooking over high heat for a few minutes, then reduce heat to a simmer. Test a grain between your thumb and forefinger: it should be soft on the outside but still a little firm. Drain the rice in a colander.

Now make the bottom crust, the all-important hakouka. Rinse and dry the pan and return it to the heat. Heat the vegetable oil until sizzling and fry the onion until soft and transparent. Pour in one tablespoon of saffron water. Then, with a slotted spoon, gradually layer the rice (this avoids compressing the grains) into the bottom of the pan. When the last of the rice is spooned on, pour over the remaining saffron water.

Lay a sheet of foil over the pan, then cover with the lid. Cook over high heat for about 3 minutes, until steam swells under the foil (take a quick look), then cook over low heat for 30 minutes or longer, if necessary. The goal is rice that is soft and fluffy but not mushy, with the grains separate.

For the furqa' heat the oil until sizzling and fry the onion until crispy and brown. Drain on paper towels.

Spoon out the rice, spices, and broken-up crust onto a large platter and sprinkle with the crispy onions. Serve with stews, poached meat, or simply savor on its own.

mu'adas

YELLOW RICE

Lentils and rice marry well, and there are endless variants of this nutritious dish throughout Asia and the Middle East: the popular Egyptian *kushari*, a dish of lentils, rice, macaroni, and hot tomato sauce; and *moujaddara*, the better-known Lebanese and Syrian version of mushy rice and brown lentils. In a Bengali cookbook I found a recipe for *khichuri*, which combines rice, lentils, and vegetables. Tony has been making wonderful food in my aunt's kitchen for as long as I can remember. This is a traditional recipe that he has perfected.

10½ oz basmati rice

7 oz yellow lentils

3 tbsp vegetable oil

2 medium onions, finely chopped

2 garlic cloves, crushed

½ tsp curry powder

½ tsp turmeric

salt to taste

FOR THE FURQA'

5 tbsp vegetable oil

2 onions, peeled and thinly sliced

serves 4

Wash the rice and lentils, then soak in cold water for about 30 minutes. Drain and set aside.

Heat the oil in a deep pan. Cook the onions first, then add the garlic and cook for about 1 minute. Add the rice and lentils, together with the spices. Pour in 2½ cups salted boiling water and bring the mixture to a boil, then simmer until the rice and lentils have softened and the water has been almost completely absorbed.

Lay a sheet of foil over the mixture, then cover with the lid and increase the heat until steam rises (look under the foil), then cook over low heat for about 45 minutes, or until the rice is soft and the moisture has evaporated.

For the furqa' heat the oil until sizzling and fry the onion until crispy and brown. Drain on paper towels.

Serve on a large, flat platter and speckle with the crispy onions.

Enjoy with braised lamb and *daqous* (see page 32) or simply on its own, with a dollop of yogurt.

mumawash

MUSHY RICE WITH MUNG BEANS

MUNG BEANS ARE as popular in Gulf cooking as they are in Indian and Chinese cuisine, where they are considered highly nutritious and easy to digest. I find the mung beans and rice pairing wholesome and comforting. This is typically eaten with poached lamb and *daqous* (see page 32) for a little piquancy. Don't skimp on the topping of raisins and onions as it adds a wonderful sweetness. Yogurt is optional but works well to cool and neutralize. Here the *hashou* is used both to perfume the dish during steaming and later as topping.

7 oz mung beans

1 lb 5 oz basmati rice

2 tbsp vegetable oil

1 large onion, finely chopped

1 garlic clove, crushed

1/2 tsp turmeric

1 3/4 oz butter, cubed

salt and freshly ground black
　　pepper

FOR THE HASHOU

2 tbsp vegetable oil

5 oz raisins, pre-soaked and
　　drained

1 large onion, finely chopped

pinch of lime powder and black
　　pepper

serves 6

Soak the beans for a few hours if possible or at least for 1–2 hours, then rinse and drain. Wash the rice and leave to soak for 30 minutes. Rinse until the water runs clear, then drain.

Heat the oil in a deep pan and cook the onion until soft, then add the garlic and cook for about 1 minute. Add the mung beans, then stir in the turmeric and rice. Pour in enough salted water to cover the ingredients by 3/4 inch, cover with the lid, and cook until the rice and beans have softened and absorbed the water.

When the rice has cooked, reduce the heat to very low and cover with a sheet of foil. Continue cooking until the moisture has evaporated (you'll need to look), then lay the butter on top of the rice – this will loosen the grains. Cover the rice with the foil again and steam for 15–30 minutes.

Now make the hashou topping. Heat the oil in a shallow pan and fry the raisins and onion over gentle heat until very soft. Season with the lime powder and black pepper.

Take the lid off the pan and scatter the onion and raisin topping over the rice. Cover again with the foil and allow the ingredients to infuse over very low heat until you are ready to serve.

This is typically eaten with chunks of braised lamb and daqous.

AROMATIC RICE WITH DILL AND FAVA BEANS

THIS POPULAR IRANIAN rice dish is enjoyed throughout the Gulf. Fava beans are also found all along the Mediterranean coast and are a valuable source of protein. They are even more nutritious when teamed with carbohydrates. Typically this dish is served with a meat stew, but it also makes a great all-around vegetarian dish. Dill enhances the taste of the beans and brings out the color. Use fresh or frozen beans, but skin and shell them.

10½ oz basmati rice

5–6 tbsp vegetable oil

1 onion, finely chopped

1 garlic clove, crushed

5 oz fava beans

1¾ oz fresh dill

salt and ground black pepper

serves 3–4

Wash the rice and leave to soak for 30 minutes. Rinse until the water runs clear, then drain.

Heat the oil in a deep pan and soften the onion and garlic. Add the beans and stir to coat with the oil mixture, then add the dill and the seasoning. Add the rice and stir the ingredients together.

Pour in enough boiling water to cover the ingredients. Cook, uncovered, over medium heat until the water has been absorbed, then reduce the heat to very low and cover with a sheet of foil, then with the lid. Steam until the moisture has evaporated.

As a vegetarian option, serve with Greek yogurt or a vegetable stew. This is also delicious with lamb or chicken.

muhammar

DATE-SWEETENED RICE

FOR ENERGY, the pearl divers traditionally ate rice sweetened with *dibs* (date-syrup) to accompany the fish they caught on those endless, arduous sea voyages on the *dhows*. Dibs was used as an alternative to sugar. These days, muhammar is still served as an accompaniment to fish dishes, but on festive occasions it may be served with a roast leg of lamb. This is seriously sweet rice, contrasting perfectly with fish, and just how the locals like it. Honey is a good substitute for the dibs.

14 oz basmati rice

pinch of saffron strands

1½ c date syrup (dibs)

1 cinnamon stick

2 cardamom pods

1 tbsp rosewater

serves 4

Wash the rice and leave to soak for 30 minutes. Rinse until the water runs clear, then drain.

Soak the saffron strands in 3–4 tablespoons of warm water for 30 minutes.

In a large pot, combine the dibs with 3⅓ cups boiling water, stirring continuously. Stir in the cinnamon stick and cardamom pods.

Add the rice and cook vigorously until the water has been absorbed. Pour the saffron and its soaking liquid together with the rosewater over the rice, then cover the pot with a sheet of foil, cover with the lid, and steam over low heat for at least 15 minutes, or until the rice grains are cooked.

Spoon out on to a large platter and top with lamb or fish.

fish and meat

machbous laham wi daqous
FRAGRANT LAMB PILAF WITH DAQOUS

THE AROMATIC MACHBOUS (*kabsa* in Saudi Arabia and Qatar) epitomizes Gulf cooking. It is a cross between a risotto and a biryani. The spiced water used to cook the meat or fish is reused to cook the rice, marrying the spices and ingredients perfectly. A machbous is enjoyed frequently but especially at family gatherings on Fridays. With the daqous adding color and a fruity piquancy, the result is highly perfumed and absolutely delicious. A glass of buttermilk is the ideal accompaniment.

Similar to a fiery Mexican salsa, daqous is a must with rice-based dishes, especially those coupled with meat or fish. I love its fruity moisture and the dash of heat that cuts through the richness of the food. I prefer to use peeled tomatoes for a smooth finish. You will need to vary the quantity of garlic and chili to taste. Bahraini daqous is made with tamarind.

10½ oz basmati rice

pinch of saffron strands

1lb 9 oz lamb, on the
    bone, cut into pieces

2 cardamom pods

1 cinnamon stick

1 bay leaf

1 clove

1 in piece ginger root

1 large onion, halved (one half
    left whole, one chopped)

3 tbsp vegetable oil

FOR THE HASHOU

2 tbsp vegetable oil

1 large onion, finely chopped

1 dried lime (lumi), very finely
    chopped or 1 tbsp lime juice

handful raisins

Wash the rice and leave to soak for 30 minutes. Rinse until the water runs clear, then drain. Soak the saffron strands in 4 tablespoons of warm water for 30 minutes.

Make the hashou. Heat the oil and fry the onion until soft, then stir in the lime and the raisins (they cook quickly) and drain all on paper towels. Set aside.

Cook the meat twice: bring a large pan of salted water to a boil, add the lamb, and cook for about 10 minutes, then drain. Refill the pan with boiling water to cover the meat by ¾ inch, add the cardamom, cinnamon, bay leaf, clove, ginger, and the whole onion half. Bring to a boil, then simmer until the meat is tender (about 1 hour 30 minutes). Remove the meat and set aside. Using a colander, drain the cooking water into a bowl and save it.

In a large saucepan heat the oil, then add the meat. Brown it but do not cook it through. Remove the meat and set aside.

In the same oil, fry the chopped onion half until lightly golden then add the rice and stir well to coat. Pour in 1¾ cups of the meat broth and bring to a boil. Cook the rice, covered, for about 15 minutes until soft but not completely cooked. Transfer 2 ladlefuls of the rice to a deep bowl and mix in the saffron water; the rice will turn yellow.

FOR THE DAQOUS

4–5 tomatoes, skinned and
   roughly chopped

¼ tsp chili powder

1 garlic clove, minced

salt to taste

serves 4

Spread the rice evenly on the bottom of the pan. Put the yellow saffron rice on the left side of the pan, lay the meat in the middle, and lastly, place the hashou on the right side of the pan. Cover with a sheet of foil and increase the heat for a minute or so until steam appears (check), then replace the lid on the pan, reduce the heat and steam for about 20–30 minutes.

To make the daqous, purée the tomatoes in a blender, then press through a fine sieve into a small saucepan. Discard any solids.

Transfer the purée to a pan and mix in the chili, garlic, and seasoning. Cook over a low heat for about 20 minutes.

You could also use canned chopped tomatoes in juice and cook everything together first, then purée. Either way, aim for a smooth texture.

When you are ready to serve the machbous, spoon the contents of the pan onto a platter, sprinkle with crispy onions, and serve with the daqous.

kabab laham
LAMB KEBABS

THE PERSIANS ARE to thank for these succulent kebabs. In the eighth century they had the excellent idea of wrapping minced meat around long skewers and grilling it over an open flame. The result was pure meat heaven and now the kebab is a universal favorite. This recipe was a well-kept secret, which I owe to my friend Nada and her family. The meat is also delicious grilled or pan-fried.

1lb 2 oz ground lamb

FOR THE MARINADE
2 tbsp Worcestershire sauce
3 slices white toast, crusts removed and processed into breadcrumbs
$1/2$ tsp oregano
1 tsp garlic purée
1 heaping tbsp ginger purée
pinch of saffron strands
$1/2$ tsp salt
$3/4$ oz melted butter
1 medium onion, finely chopped
1 tsp fresh parsley, chopped
1 egg, beaten

serves 4

Place the meat in a large bowl and add all the marinade ingredients. Mix together, using your hands or in a food processor. The meat should feel firm but slightly sticky.

Scoop up palm-sized quantities of the meat and, using both hands, mold upwards, not too thinly, into 2 inch long, $1/2$ inch thick kebabs. If cooking over charcoal, thread the meat on to long, thick skewers. If the meat is too sticky, sprinkle a little flour over it to make it easier to handle.

Cook over a barbecue or charcoal fire, turning the skewers occasionally, for about 5 minutes. Otherwise spread the kebabs on a tray under the grill for about 5–8 minutes, turning them over once. They are also good pan-fried in very little oil.

Eat with a salad or in pita bread. In the Gulf, kebabs are traditionally served with fragrant basmati rice topped with ruby-red barberries.

marag shabzi
LAMB AND HERB STEW

SHABZI, OR SABZI in Persian, is a bunch of fresh herbs. I was taught to make this by a Kuwaiti friend of Iranian descent. In the Gulf you can buy sorted, tied bunches of fresh herbs from the grocer. You can also use canned sabzi that can be found at Persian grocers, which cuts preparation time and tastes just as good. I strongly recommend this shortcut. But you can also do it the traditional way, using fresh herbs.

1 lb 5 oz lamb pieces,
   on the bone
1 cinnamon stick
2 cardamom pods
1 clove
½ tsp black peppercorns
1 garlic clove, peeled
2½ oz black-eyed beans
   or red kidney beans
3 tbsp vegetable oil
2 medium onions, finely
   chopped
2 garlic cloves, crushed
2 large tomatoes, diced
3 dried limes (lumi)
1 whole green chili
1 tsp dried lime powder or
   1 tbsp lime or lemon juice
salt to taste
15-oz can sabzi or 5 oz parsley,
   5 oz dill, 5 oz cilantro or
   parsley and 2 oz fresh or
   2 tbsp dried fenugreek

serves 6

If you can't get hold of canned sabzi, use fresh herbs as follows: wash and dry each bunch of herbs and then chop roughly. Place in a food processor and blend with just enough oil to make a thick, dark paste.

Trim the meat of any excess fat then cook it twice. Bring a large pan of salted water to a boil, add the lamb, and cook for about 15 minutes, then drain off the water. Refill the pan with boiling water, add the meat, the spices, and garlic clove and cook for about 1 hour 30 minutes, or until very tender. Drain the meat, save the cooking liquid, and discard the spices.

Wash the beans, then cover in salted boiling water and cook for 15 minutes. Drain and set aside.

Heat the oil in a large pan, then add the onion and cook until soft. Stir in the crushed garlic and cook for 2 minutes or so, then add the meat and stir to coat. Add the tomatoes and cook over medium heat while they soften and liquidize.

Puncture each dried lime twice with a knife and place in the pan together with the whole chili and dried lime powder or lime or lemon juice. Pour in enough of the cooking water to cover the meat by 5/8 inch. Stir in the sabzi or herb and oil mixture and the beans (if you like, add some roasted potato chunks). Season with salt to taste. Cook for 40 minutes or until the stew is thick. To reduce the sauce cook a little while longer over medium heat.

Serve in bowls, with rice.

 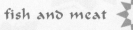

batata chab
POTATO "CHOPS"

THE BENGALIS ARE famous for their "chops," potato croquettes eaten as snacks with tea. These perfect orange potato cakes are delicious and filling. In the Gulf, they go by the Arabized name *batata chab*, and in our family they were unfailingly dished up by my aunt as a snack when family and friends came around for afternoon tea, and at my dad's weekly *diwaniyya*.

2 tbsp vegetable oil, plus extra for deep-frying

3 medium onions, finely chopped

9 oz lean lamb or ground beef

2 garlic cloves, crushed

2 lb 4 oz potatoes (about 4 medium potatoes), peeled and quartered

3½ oz basmati rice

pinch of turmeric

2 eggs, beaten

breadcrumbs for coating

salt and pepper to taste

serves 6

Heat the oil in a large saucepan, then fry the onion and meat. Halfway through add the garlic. When the meat is cooked, set it aside.

Cook the potatoes in a large pan of boiling water until very tender (15–20 minutes, depending on the variety). Transfer them to a bowl and mash with a fork. In another pan of boiling water slightly over-cook the rice until soft and sticky.

Combine the potatoes with the rice and add the turmeric. Season to taste. Blend the ingredients together either by hand or with a potato masher until the mixture is smooth.

Take up egg-sized portions of the potato mixture into the palm of your hand. Flatten out against the curve of your palm and fill with half a teaspoon of the meat. Gently fold the potato over and around the meat into a round patty. The meat should be enclosed.

Dip the potato cakes into the beaten eggs, then coat with breadcrumbs. Fry in hot oil in batches until they are evenly brown. Drain on paper towels.

Best eaten warm, as a snack with sweet black tea or dipped in daqous.

biryani diyay
CHICKEN BIRYANI

BIRYANI ORIGINATED at the imperial court of Ancient Persia (the Persian for baked is *beryân*), then traveled east to emerge as the star of Indian subcontinental cuisine. This is majestic food – a combination to charm and bewilder the senses. This recipe was given to me by Hamza, a South Indian chef who has worked in Bahrain for many years.

pinch of saffron strands

1½ lb chicken, cut
    into 6–8 pieces

1 large potato, sliced into thick
    rounds

3 tsp Madras curry powder

salt to taste

1½ c vegetable oil

3 onions, finely chopped

2¾ oz cashew nuts

2¾ oz raisins

1½ garlic cloves, chopped

½ tbsp ginger root, chopped

½ green chili, seeded and
    finely chopped

2 medium tomatoes, roughly
    chopped

1 tsp cilantro, chopped

7 oz plain yogurt

1 tbsp rosewater

FOR THE RICE

11 oz basmati rice

1 cinnamon stick

3 cloves

3 cardamom pods

salt to taste

serves 4

Soak the saffron in 4 tablespoons of warm water for 30 minutes. Rub the chicken pieces and potato with two teaspoons of curry powder and some salt. Wash the rice and leave to soak for 30 minutes. Rinse until the water runs clear, then drain.

Heat the oil in a large pan and deep-fry half the onion until soft. Drain on paper towels. In the same oil fry the cashews, then the raisins (be careful, they cook very fast) until lightly golden, then transfer to paper towels. Increase the heat to medium and put in the chicken until the skin browns. Remove and place in a separate, deep pan. Partially fry the potatoes until lightly golden – this will take about 8 minutes – then place them on top of the chicken. Fry the remaining onion, garlic, ginger, and green chili for 2 minutes. Add the tomato, the remaining curry powder, and salt to taste. Cook until the tomatoes liquidize, then stir in the cilantro and yogurt and remove from the heat. Pour the sauce over the pieces of chicken and potato, cover and cook over low heat for about 45 minutes.

About 10 minutes before the chicken and potatoes are cooked, bring the same amount of water as rice to a boil. Add the spices and some salt. Cook the rice until soft and the water has been absorbed.

Sprinkle a layer of rice into another deep pan and top with the chicken, potatoes, and the sauce. Sprinkle over the fried raisins, cashews, and onion and top with the remaining rice. Pour the rosewater and saffron water over the rice.

Lay a sheet of foil over the biryani, replace the lid, and return to the heat. Cook over high heat for a minute until steam rises. Reduce the heat and steam for about 15 minutes.

Serve with a side of yogurt and chopped cucumbers.

kabab diyay
BREADED CHICKEN KEBABS

THESE ARE ANOTHER great snack option. Excellent with a glass of sweet black tea, they are often served up along with potato "chops" and *sambousa* (samosas) in the afternoon. They are quick and easy to make and taste delicious; also good with a mixed salad.

2 lb 4 oz ground chicken

4 oz cilantro or parsley

2 red onions, roughly chopped

4 heaping tbsp breadcrumbs

8 garlic cloves, chopped

¹/₂ tsp cumin

¹/₂ tsp turmeric

¹/₂ tsp salt

¹/₂ tsp black pepper

I c heavy cream

7 tbsp vegetable oil

serves 4

In a large bowl combine the ground chicken with the herbs, onions, breadcrumbs, spices, salt, pepper, cream, and oil. Mix the ingredients together. The meat should feel supple but firm enough to shape.

Scoop up palm-sized quantities of the mixture. On a chopping board roll the meat out and away from you, shaping it into medium-sized sausage-like rolls that are neither too chunky nor too thin.

Dip each kebab in egg and breadcrumbs to coat and fry in hot vegetable oil, in batches, until they turn golden brown. Remove with a slotted spoon and drain on paper towels.

Alternatively, add two eggs to the chicken mixture and cook the kebabs under a hot grill.

Serve warm with pita bread and a salad.

diyay mahshi bil tamr

CHICKEN WITH DATE, PRUNE, AND NUT STUFFING

MOROCCAN CUISINE is the inspiration behind this dazzling dish. The combination of sweet and savory ingredients is common to Moroccan cooking, as it is to Gulf food. In Morocco, dried fruits like prunes and apricots are used, while in the Gulf it is dates and raisins. The chopped nuts are a wonderful contrast to the sweet fruit and the simplicity of the chicken meat. The stuffing is delicious on its own.

1 whole chicken

FOR THE MARINADE
3 tbsp barbecue sauce
1/2 tsp turmeric
1 tsp salt

FOR THE STUFFING
3 tbsp walnuts
2 tbsp almonds
3 tbsp pine nuts
2 tbsp vegetable oil
1 small onion, finely chopped
1 tomato, finely chopped
1 1/2 tsp barbecue sauce
2 tbsp lemon juice
9 oz prunes, roughly chopped
9 oz dates, roughly chopped
3 tbsp cooked rice (any type)
salt to taste

serves 4

Preheat the oven to 400°F (200°C).

Mix the marinade ingredients together, coat the chicken with it and set aside.

Make the stuffing. First, break the nuts up. Mohamed, the cook who showed me this recipe, packed the nuts into a small plastic bag and banged it a few times against the kitchen work surface, which nicely broke the nuts up without having to use a knife.

Heat the oil in a large saucepan and cook the onion until soft and transparent. Add the nuts, tomato, barbecue sauce, and lemon juice, and stir. Cook for a few minutes, or until the tomatoes begin to liquidize. Remove from the heat and add the prunes and dates together with the cooked rice. Combine well, adding salt to taste. Firmly pack the stuffing into the chicken's cavity and tie with string.

 fish and meat

Place the chicken in a roasting dish and cook for
30 minutes, then reduce the temperature to 350°F (180°C)
and cook for another 30 minutes. If the chicken skin starts to
blacken, cover with a sheet of foil and return to the oven.

The nuttiness and sweetness of this dish make brown rice
the perfect accompaniment.

mtabag simach
ULTIMATE FISH ON RICE

THE ZUBAIDI (silver pomfret) is the most revered of local fish varieties and is a mainstay of the fishing industry. Its flesh is white and flaky. I have memories of my father scooping out parcels of rice and hashou with bits of this white fish meat. He ate this with his fingers, which is the customary (and most personally satisfying) way of enjoying this dish. In the Gulf, the silver pomfret is only found in the coastal waters of Iran, Iraq, and Kuwait.

1 silver pomfret, Chilean sea
    bass, or any firm white fish
11 oz basmati rice
1 cinnamon stick
2 cardamom pods
2 cloves
salt and pepper

FOR THE HASHOU
3 tbsp vegetable oil
2 onions, finely chopped
1 tsp cilantro, roughly
    chopped
1/2 tsp dried lime powder or
    2 tbsp lemon juice
1/4 tsp salt
1/4 tsp pepper

FOR THE TOPPING
1 tbsp vegetable oil
1 onion, finely chopped
pinch of turmeric
pinch of dried lime powder
    (or as above)
salt and pepper to taste

serves 4

Ask your fish dealer to clean and gut the fish for you. Rinse well, then rub it with salt. Wash the rice and leave to soak for 30 minutes. Rinse until the water runs clear, then drain.

Bring a large pan of water to a boil. Put in the fish and the spices and boil until cooked. Remove the fish and set aside, saving the cooking water by draining into a large bowl through a colander.

Make the hashou. Heat the oil and sauté the onion until soft and golden, add the cilantro, lime powder or lemon juice, and seasoning, and blend well. When the fish is cool enough to handle, pack this stuffing into the fish's cavity and stitch it up.

Heat some oil in a large saucepan. Fry the fish, turning it occasionally, until golden brown, then drain it on paper towels and set aside. Frying the fish, having already cooked it, may seem superfluous but it adds to the flavor.

Pour 2 cups of the fish cooking water into a large, deep pan and bring to a boil. Add the rice, cover, and cook until the rice softens and the water has been absorbed.

Meanwhile, fry the topping ingredients in the oil.

When the rice is cooked, lay the fish over it to one side of the pan. Place the onion topping on the other side. This juxtaposition allows all the flavors to infuse together. Put the pan back on the heat and cover with a sheet of foil, then with the lid. Increase the heat to high (take a look to check that steam is rising underneath the foil), then reduce to the lowest setting and steam for at least 30 minutes, ideally 1 hour.

Spoon the rice and topping out on to a large plate and place the fish on top. Serve with yogurt or daqous (see page 32).

 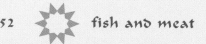

marag simach/matfi
AROMATIC FISH STEW

THIS POPULAR fish stew is served in honor of special guests. The *hamour* (brown-spotted grouper) is another much-prized local Arabian fish, and a staple at banquets. Very high in protein, its chunky white flesh lends itself beautifully to spices. My fish dealer suggested bream, haddock, cod, or turbot in place of the hamour used in this traditional stew.

2 lb 4 oz hamour or other fish,
    cut into chunks
1 tsp all-purpose flour

FOR THE MARINADE
2 garlic cloves, crushed
3 tbsp lemon juice
½ in piece ginger root,
    finely chopped
salt and pepper

1 walnut-sized piece tamarind
    or 1 tsp tamarind paste
2 dried limes (lumi) or 2 tbsp
    lime juice
3 tbsp vegetable oil for frying
2 medium onions, finely
    chopped
1 green chili, halved lengthways
1 tsp cumin seeds
1 tsp dried lime powder or
    2 tbsp lemon or lime juice
2 medium tomatoes, roughly
    chopped
1 tbsp tomato purée
1 tbsp fresh dill, chopped
2 tbsp cilantro, chopped
salt and pepper to taste

serves 4

Wash the fish pieces and let dry. Rub them first with the flour then coat them in the marinade ingredients. Season with salt and pepper and allow to stand for at least 30 minutes, preferably longer.

If making your own past, remove any seeds from the tamarind and leave it to soak in 1 cup warm water.

Puncture each dried lime a few times with a sharp knife. Fry the fish in the oil in a large saucepan until nicely golden, then drain on a paper towels. In the same oil, fry the onion until soft and transparent, then add the green chili and spices. Stir for about 1 minute before adding the tomatoes, tomato purée, dill, and dried limes.

Strain the tamarind paste into the stew (or add 1 teaspoon tamarind paste) and cook for a few more minutes before adding the fish pieces. Mix in the cilantro and season to taste.

Allow the stew to simmer for at least 15 minutes. Serve with mashkhoul (see page 21).

hamour mahshi

BAKED FISH WITH NUT STUFFING

IN OLDEN TIMES, fish was inexpensive in the Gulf. Red meat was only eaten occasionally and chicken was an expensive delicacy. The hamour was then a poor person's fish. These days it is considered one of the Arabian Sea's prize catches and goes for a small fortune at the fishmarket. It is especially impressive served on a bed of fragrant yellow and white rice. Try this recipe with seabass or cod.

I whole hamour

I¹/₂ tsp turmeric

salt to taste

3 garlic cloves, crushed

I in piece ginger root,
  finely chopped

I tsp cumin

¹/₂ tsp black pepper

salt to taste

2 tbsp vegetable oil

2 large onions, I chopped
  and I sliced

I³/₄ oz almonds,
  roughly chopped

³/₄ oz pine nuts,
  roughly chopped

³/₄ oz walnuts, roughly
  chopped

2 tbsp barbecue sauce

2 tbsp ketchup

2 tsp soy sauce

I tsp cilantro, roughly chopped

I large potato, sliced into
  rounds

serves 4

Preheat the oven to 400°F (200°C).

Wash the fish, descale it, cut off the fins and tail, and slice it down the middle to remove the insides. Alternatively, ask your fish dealer to clean and gut the fish for you. Rub it with I teaspoon of the turmeric and some salt and set it aside for about I hour, then rinse off any coloring.

Blend the crushed garlic and chopped ginger, cumin, the remaining turmeric, black pepper, and salt together into a paste. Set aside. Heat the vegetable oil in a large saucepan and fry I chopped onion until soft and transparent. Stir in the nuts, barbecue sauce, ketchup, and the soy sauce. Add the garlic-ginger paste and the chopped cilantro and stir over heat for a few minutes, then remove from heat.

Line a large rectangular baking tray with foil. Spread out a layer of potato slices, then top with the onion slices. Stuff the fish firmly with the nut mixture, then stitch it up. Place it over the potato and onion in the tray.

Bake the fish for 30–40 minutes, or until done. If the skin starts to blacken, cover with a sheet of foil.

Serve immediately.

mrabyan

SHRIMP AND RICE

THOUGH CRUSTACEA and seafood are not traditionally eaten in the Gulf, shrimp are the exception. The variety caught in the waters off the Arabian coast are fleshy and plump, perfect for cooking. Shrimp are so popular they are often over-fished, and every year or so a ban is imposed to allow them time to regenerate. This is a wonderfully fragrant biryani.

14 oz shrimp

juice of 1 lemon

1 tsp turmeric

1 tsp salt

1 lb 9 oz basmati rice

1 vegetable stock cube

5 tbsp vegetable oil

1 cinnamon stick

5 cardamom pods

5 cloves

6 garlic cloves, chopped

1½ in piece ginger root,
    finely sliced

6 small red onions, thinly
    sliced

1 small green pepper, chopped

1 tsp cumin

1 tsp Madras curry powder

3 large tomatoes, chopped

1 tbsp tomato purée

1 small potato, peeled and
    diced

1 large potato, peeled and
    sliced into ¼ in rounds

1 tsp cilantro, roughly chopped

serves 8

Rinse the shrimp thoroughly. Remove the head and tail, then soak in the juice of half a lemon for 15 minutes or so. De-vein the shrimp using a sharp knife and rinse well. Sprinkle with ½ teaspoon each of turmeric and salt, then set aside.

Wash the rice and leave to soak for 30 minutes. Rinse until the water runs clear, then drain.

Place the vegetable stock cube in a large pan and pour 4 cups water to dissolve. Bring to a boil. Add the shrimp – they will get plump and glossy within minutes. Drain and set aside.

Heat 3 tablespoons of vegetable oil in a large pan over medium heat. Fry the cinnamon, cardamom, and cloves to bring out their flavor, then add the garlic and ginger and cook until the garlic is lightly golden. Add the onion and green pepper and cook for a few minutes.

Add the shrimp to the onion and spices. Stir in the cumin and curry powder as well as the remaining turmeric and salt to taste. Put in the chopped tomatoes, the remaining lemon juice, the tomato purée, and 1 cup water. Cover the pan and bring to a boil, then reduce heat and simmer.

Meanwhile, boil the diced potato for about 8 minutes, then toss into the bubbling shrimp mixture. Cook for a few minutes over the lowest heat. Adjust the salt, then remove from the heat.

Bring the same amount of salted water as rice to a boil and cook the rice until it is soft and the water has been absorbed.

Layer the ingredients into a deep-bottomed casserole. Spoon 2 tablespoons of vegetable oil into the bottom of the dish and place the uncooked potato slices across the bottom. Ladle over some juice from the shrimp, then sprinkle with some cilantro.

Lay a few shrimp over the potatoes, then top with a layer of rice. Top with the remaining shrimp, a final layer of rice and, lastly, the remaining cilantro.

Put the casserole dish on the stove and cover with a sheet of foil, then with the lid. Cook over high heat for about 1 minute (take a look to check if steam is rising), then reduce to the lowest setting and steam for 20 minutes.

Spoon out onto a large platter. Serve with daqous or yogurt.

vegetables

shilla

GRAINS AND SPINACH PORRIDGE

SHILLA IS A Persian-inspired, throw-it-all-in savory porridge. In the old days, this dish would feed large numbers of people, usually an extended family. Generous quantities would be made in the morning and cooked for up to half a day. Before serving, the vat would be placed on the kitchen floor and the cook would sit astride it and beat the mixture smooth with a large wooden spoon. In spite of today's modern conveniences, shilla and the porridges in the following recipes are still made in the traditional way.

3¹/₂ oz mung beans

3¹/₂ oz basmati rice

3¹/₂ oz green lentils

2 tbsp vegetable oil

I large onion, finely chopped

2 garlic cloves, crushed

I in piece ginger root,
    finely chopped

I tsp Madras curry powder

I tsp turmeric

I tsp cumin

I large tomato, skinned and
    roughly chopped

7 oz spinach or Swiss chard

salt to taste

I vegetable stock cube

crispy onions, to serve

serves 6

Soak the mung beans overnight if possible, otherwise for a couple of hours. Drain before cooking. Wash the rice and lentils and soak for 30 minutes, then drain.

Heat the vegetable oil in a large, deep pan and fry the onion until lightly golden. Add the garlic, ginger, and the spices and stir well. Stir in the tomato and spinach and season with salt to taste.

Allow the spinach to soften, then add the mung beans, lentils, and rice, and cover with 3¼ cups boiling water. Bring to a boil, then reduce heat and simmer gently for about 55 minutes. Stir the mixture every 15 minutes or so as it cooks and if it starts to stick to the bottom of the pan, add some water. Halfway through crumble in the stock cube.

Shortly before serving, whip the mixture until well blended. To do this use either a whisk or hand mixer.

Spoon out into a large serving bowl and sprinkle with crispy onions; thick yogurt goes well too.

jareesh

CRACKED WHEAT AND VEGETABLES

JAREESH IS COARSE cracked wheat, cleaned and crushed, resembling bulgur. In the past, it was the poor person's rice. During the second world war, the disruption of trade and the scarcity of rice meant that people used jareesh (probably farmed in neighboring Iraq) as an alternative. This versatile dish is still cooked today, especially at Ramadhan. Almost any root vegetable can be used in place of those listed: turnips and sweet potatoes both work well. This is healthy, hearty comfort food. It tastes equally good with lamb or chicken.

14 oz jareesh (wheat, cleaned and crushed)

2 tbsp tomato purée

2 tbsp olive oil

salt to taste

2 tbsp vegetable oil

2 medium onions, finely chopped

1 cinnamon stick

3–4 cloves

½ tsp ginger purée

1 carrot, sliced into rounds

1 zucchini, sliced into rounds

1 small green pepper, sliced in half and diced

1 medium potato, peeled and cubed

3½ oz green beans, diced

3½ oz green peas

3 medium tomatoes, chopped

½ tsp turmeric

2 tbsp lemon juice

serves 8

Rinse the wheat several times, as you would rice, and drain to remove any impurities. Squeeze out any excess water then place in a bowl. Stir in half the tomato purée, the olive oil, and some salt and combine well using a wooden spoon.

Heat the vegetable oil in a heavy-bottomed pan and fry the onion until soft and translucent. Stir in the spices and ginger purée.

Add all the vegetables and tomatoes to the pan and cook over low heat for a minute or so, then add some salt, the turmeric, and the remaining tomato purée. Combine well.

Pour 1 cup water into the pan and cook over medium heat for about 15 minutes, or until the potato is almost cooked (test with a knife). Lay a sheet of foil over the mixture and cover with the lid (take a look to make sure steam is rising), then add the lemon juice.

When the vegetables are tender, remove them from the pan and set aside. Add the jareesh and ½ cup water and bring to a boil. Keep stirring as the wheat thickens, then remove from the heat.

Layer the ingredients in a deep casserole dish: sprinkle the wheat onto the bottom, then top with a layer of vegetables. Repeat twice.

Put the casserole dish on the stove, lay a sheet of foil over the mixture, and cover with the lid. Steam over low heat for 55 minutes. Serve in a large bowl.

madhrouba
"BEATEN" PORRIDGE

THIS RAMADHAN FAVORITE is wintry and warming as well as an excellent all-year-rounder. During lean times in the past, people cooked with barley, lentils, and coarse, cracked wheat as they were locally farmed, highly nutritious, and inexpensive. Today if I'm in the mood for something healthy and wholesome, I throw the ingredients together in a pot in the morning and let them cook throughout the day. The hashou is sprinkled over the top as garnish.

9 oz jareesh

3 tbsp vegetable oil

1 large onion, finely chopped

3 garlic cloves, crushed

$\frac{1}{2}$ in piece ginger root,
   finely chopped

7 oz boneless chicken,
   chopped into bite-sized
   chunks

2 medium tomatoes, skinned
   and roughly chopped

1 tsp Madras curry powder

1 tsp cumin

$\frac{1}{2}$ tsp turmeric

1 tsp cilantro, chopped

salt to taste

FOR THE HASHOU

2 small onions, finely chopped

$\frac{1}{2}$ tsp dried lime powder or
   2 tbsp lime juice

1 bunch cilantro, finely
   chopped

2 tbsp vegetable oil

serves 6

Wash the wheat well to remove any impurities. Rinse several times, squeeze out any excess water, then place in a bowl.

Heat the oil in a large, deep pan. Sauté the onion until soft, then add the garlic and ginger. Put in the chicken and cook for a few minutes to brown, then add the tomatoes, spices, and cilantro and stir until the tomatoes start to liquidize.

Add the drained wheat and $3\frac{1}{4}$ cups boiling water. Cover and cook over low heat for 2–3 hours. Season with salt to taste. Stir the mixture every 30 minutes or so. When cooked the meat and wheat should be so well combined they are hard to tell apart.

Fry the hashou ingredients in the oil and set aside.

At the end of the cooking process beat the madhrouba until smooth. I used an hand mixer, which did the task well but didn't produce my aunt's manually-beaten smoothness. Nevertheless, the dish tasted every bit as delicious, beaten smooth or not.

Pour into a large platter and garnish with the hashou.

shorbat 'adas

DIVINE LENTIL SOUP

SHORBAT 'ADAS or shorbat al-dal, as it is also known, is the quintessential Middle Eastern soup. My aunt is famous for hers, particularly during Ramadhan, when she ladles it out daily to scores of relatives and fast-breakers. The tradition is to start with a date (to regulate blood-sugar levels after the long, daily fast) and follow with a restorative bowl of dal. This recipe is nutritious and satisfying. The cooked limes, or lumi, are the secret ingredient. Squeeze one against the side of your serving bowl to release the tart juice. Variations of this soup exist across the region and throughout the Indian subcontinent.

7 oz red lentils

4 medium tomatoes, skinned
    and roughly chopped

3 dried limes (lumi) or 3 tbsp
    lime juice

4 tbsp vegetable oil

3 medium onions, finely
    chopped

½ tsp garlic purée

½ tsp ginger purée

½ tsp Madras curry powder

½ tsp turmeric

½ tsp cumin

2 tbsp tomato purée

2 vermicelli nests or
    1¾ oz shredded vermicelli

salt to taste

serves 6–8

Rinse the lentils until the water runs clear. Put them in a large pan and add 2¼ cups boiling water. Bring to a boil, then simmer, covered, until the lentils are soft. Add the chopped tomatoes and cook for about 5 minutes.

Blend the mixture in batches in a blender or food processor. Set aside.

Pierce each dried lime a few times with a knife. Heat the oil in another deep pan and fry the onion and the dried limes together until the onion is golden brown. Stir in the garlic and ginger purées and the spices.

Combine the lentil mixture with the onion mixture, stir well, and season with salt to taste. Add the tomato purée. Cook over medium heat until the mixture starts to bubble.

Lastly, add the vermicelli. When they are cooked – within 3 minutes – the soup is ready. Adjust the consistency by adding water, if necessary.

Pour into soup bowls, and don't forget the limes.

marag dal
RED LENTIL STEW

THIS IS AN EVERYDAY DISH – healthy, nutritious, and easy to make. Its vibrant orange color and green garnish make it attractive to put before friends. It's also very tasty.

1 lb 2 oz red lentils

2 potatoes, peeled and cubed

2 onions, finely chopped

3 tbsp vegetable oil

2 garlic cloves, crushed

2 large tomatoes, roughly
  chopped

1/2 tsp turmeric

1 tsp cilantro, roughly chopped

salt and pepper to taste

serves 4

Rinse the lentils until the water runs clear, then drain.

Put the lentils in a large pan, add enough boiling water to cover by 1/2 inch and bring to a boil. Reduce the heat to low and simmer for about a minute, then add the potato and half the chopped onion and cover with the lid. Simmer for about 15 minutes, or until the lentils are soft and mushy and the potato is cooked. Season to taste.

Heat the oil in a deep pan and fry the remaining onion with the garlic until the onion softens. Pour in 3/4 cup boiling water and stir in the chopped tomatoes and the turmeric. Cook over medium heat until the water reduces and the mixture thickens. Season to taste and set aside.

Whip the lentil and potato mixture for a minute or so using a whisk or hand mixer. Combine well with the tomato mixture, then remove the pan from the heat. Check the seasoning.

Garnish with a generous sprinkling of chopped cilantro. Serve with rice or warm pita bread.

foul

CRUSHED SPICED FAVA BEANS

THIS MOUTHWATERING recipe comes from my friend's mother, Afaf. *Foul* (pronounced 'fool') are fava beans. Egyptians adore them, eat them almost every day, and use them to make tasty *ta'miyya* falafels. They are the iconic Arab popular food. Cans of foul line the shelves of Middle Eastern grocers the world over. High in protein, inexpensive, and extremely versatile, the beans can be cooked just about any way. In the Gulf, foul is sometimes eaten for breakfast or as a side dish at lunch or dinner. I love this recipe's tartness, thanks to plenty of cilantro and lemon juice, which give the legumes a nice lift. Count one can per person.

2 tbsp olive oil

2 medium tomatoes, skinned
and cubed

4–5 tsp cilantro,
roughly chopped

½ tsp cumin

2 cans (1 lb) foul (fava beans)

4 tbsp lemon juice

chili powder to taste

salt and pepper to taste

FOR THE GARNISH

olive oil for drizzling

1 tsp cilantro, roughly chopped

1 small tomato, diced

serves 2

Heat the oil in a pan and cook the tomatoes for a few minutes until they start to soften and liquidize. Stir in the chopped cilantro and cumin.

Pour the contents of the cans of foul through a fine sieve, draining any excess liquid, then add the beans to the tomatoes. Cook for a few minutes and, as you stir, mash up a few beans against the edge of the pan to make the mixture creamy. Season to taste. Add the lemon juice and chili powder and season to taste.

Before serving, drizzle with olive oil and garnish with chopped cilantro and diced tomato. Devour warm with toasted pita bread.

marag fasoolya

GREEN BEAN STEW

BAMYA (OKRA) and fasoolya (green beans) are some of the most popular vegetable stews in the Gulf and throughout the Middle East. Stews are so simple and quick to make. A few ingredients and spices from the pantry will do the trick as long as fresh vegetables are available. This recipe can be used with a variety of different vegetables.

9 oz green beans

2 tbsp olive oil

2 small onions, finely sliced

1 large garlic clove, chopped

1 in piece ginger root,
    finely chopped

½ tsp turmeric

½ tsp curry powder

4 tomatoes, skinned and
    roughly chopped

1 tbsp tomato purée

salt to taste

1 bunch cilantro, roughly
    chopped

serves 4

Wash and trim the beans.

Heat the oil in a large saucepan and fry the onion slices until soft and transparent. Add the garlic and ginger, and cook for about 1 minute. Stir in the turmeric and curry powder.

Add the tomatoes and stir for a few minutes over low heat, until the tomatoes start to liquidize. Add ¾ cup boiling water, then throw in the beans and cook until tender. Add the tomato purée and salt to taste.

Garnish with chopped cilantro and serve warm with rice or bread.

tashreeba

"THE DRINKER"

THE ROOT OF the word *tashreeba* is *sharaba*, to drink. This dish gets its name from the way the bread (usually the wafer-thin kind) soaks up the cooking juices and swells into something resembling pasta ribbons. The stew (also known as *thareed* in Bahrain and Qatar) is traditionally made with pumpkin or potato but I often use butternut squash. In Kuwait people make this a complete meal by adding chunks of lamb or chicken. This is another favorite during Ramadhan. Use pita if you cannot find wafer bread.

1 quantity of daqous
   (see page 32)

3 tbsp vegetable oil

1 large onion, finely chopped

1 large garlic clove, crushed

1/2 in piece ginger root,
   finely chopped

1/2 tsp cumin

1 tsp curry powder

1/4 tsp turmeric

3 dried limes (lumi) or 3 tbsp
   lime juice

1 tbsp tomato purée (optional)

9 oz butternut squash,
   roughly chopped

1 packet khubz rqaq (wafer
   bread) or similar thin flat
   bread

FOR THE GARNISH

1 small red onion, finely
   chopped

2 tbsp cilantro, chopped

1/4 tsp dried lime powder

freshly ground black pepper

2 tbsp vegetable oil

serves 4

Prepare the daqous and set aside.

Heat the oil in a large casserole over medium heat. Add the onion and cook until soft, then add the garlic and ginger and stir for about a minute. Stir in the cumin, curry powder, turmeric, dried limes and pour in the daqous mix; check the seasoning and add salt, if necessary. Simmer for about 5 minutes (add the tomato purée to enhance the color and thicken the sauce at this stage, if you like), then pour in 2¼ cups boiling water.

Add the squash and simmer. When the squash is cooked to your liking (I prefer it al dente), remove the pan from the heat.

While the squash is cooking, prepare the garnish by sautéing the ingredients in the oil until soft. Set aside.

Tear up the wafer bread and scatter the pieces into a deep serving bowl. Pour the cooking juice over the bread and spread with a fork. The bread and juice will congeal into an orangey pasta-like dough.

Top with the squash, any remaining sauce, the dried limes, and lastly the garnish.

gaboot

DUMPLINGS, GULF-STYLE

INTRIGUINGLY REMINISCENT of the eastern European dishes, these dumplings are light and juicy with a sweet-sour stuffing. The filling is so unusual that when I first make this for friends they spend half the meal trying to guess the ingredients. Traditionally, chunks of lamb are cooked alongside the vegetables, though I prefer this lighter version. Chopped nuts (walnuts and pine nuts) are another flavorful stuffing option.

FOR THE DOUGH

9 oz all-purpose flour

$^1/_2$ cup vegetable oil

$^1/_2$ cup water

$^1/_2$ tsp salt

2 dried limes (lumi) or 2 tbsp
   lime juice

2 tbsp vegetable oil

1 onion, finely chopped

2 large garlic cloves, crushed

1 in piece ginger root,
   finely chopped

3 large tomatoes, skinned and
   roughly chopped

1 tsp tomato purée

1 large carrot, sliced into thick
   rounds

2 small zucchinis, sliced into
   thick rounds

$^1/_2$ tsp turmeric

$^1/_2$ tsp curry powder

$^1/_2$ tsp cumin

salt to taste

Mix the dough ingredients together then knead well until it no longer sticks to your fingers (if necessary, add some flour to make it easier to work). Allow the dough to rest in a cool place while you prepare the stew.

Puncture each dried lime a few times with a knife. Heat the oil in a deep pan and fry the onion and dried limes. When the onion is soft, remove the limes and set them aside. Add the garlic and ginger to the pan and cook for about 1 minute, then add the tomatoes and tomato purée.

Put in the carrots, zucchinis, and reserved limes, then pour in enough water to cover the ingredients by ¾ inch. Add the spices and some salt and cook until the vegetables are done to your liking, then remove them from the pan with a slotted spoon and set aside. Keep the cooking juices warm.

Make the hashou. Soften the onions in the oil, then add the raisins and seasoning and mix well. Set aside.

FOR THE HASHOU

2 tbsp vegetable oil

2 medium onions, finely
  chopped

1¾ oz raisins

1 tsp dried lime powder

½ tsp black pepper

serves 8

Sprinkle some flour on the work surface. Thinly roll out the dough and, with a biscuit cutter, cut out large, saucer-size rounds. Flip each round over (flour side down, sticky side up) in your palm, fill the center with 1 teaspoon of hashou, then press the two edges of the dough together into crescent shapes.

Bring the stew to a boil, then carefully drop in the dumplings. Cook them for about 2 minutes over high heat, then reduce the heat and simmer for 30 minutes, stirring occasionally. As they cook, the dumplings will flesh out and rise to the surface.

Shortly before removing the pan from the heat put the vegetables and limes back into the stew. Serve in deep bowls.

desserts

muhalbiyat al-ruz
MILKY RICE PUDDING

M Y SISTER LOVES this dessert, and as a girl she forever pestered my aunt to make it for her. Milky desserts are very popular in the Middle East, and this one is a particular favorite – the rice thickens to give it texture. There are many ways of making muhalbiya: with rice; with rice flour; or with corn flour, the way it is made in Lebanon and Syria. Top with chopped pistachios to add some color and crunch.

6 oz basmati rice

4 c whole milk

6–8 tbsp sugar

1/2 tsp green cardamom seeds, crushed

3 tbsp rosewater

handful pistachios, chopped

serves 6

Wash the rice and leave to soak for 30 minutes. Rinse until the water runs clear, then drain.

Put the rice and 1 cup cold water in a blender and process for about 3 minutes, or until the liquid becomes milky and the rice turns paste-like (this may take a few minutes depending on the variety of rice). You can also use a whisk.

Warm the milk in a casserole dish then add the sugar. Stir with a wooden spoon over high heat until bubbles form at the side of the pan, then reduce the heat and simmer for about 1 minute. Add the blended rice and cook for about 20 minutes; as you stir the mixture will thicken and you will feel resistance. Test the rice to see if it is cooked – it should be al dente.

Add another 1 cup boiling water, stir in the cardamom seeds and the rosewater, and simmer over the lowest heat for a few more minutes.

Remove from the heat and pour into bowls. Allow to cool before chilling in the refrigerator.

Serve sprinkled with chopped pistachios.

DATE FUDGE DESSERT

I WAS TAUGHT to make 'afoosa by my friend's aunt Wajeeha, in Bahrain, where she is famous for it. When I was a child it was my favorite dessert, even before I knew its name, and since then I have spent years searching for the recipe. We used Saudi dates, the soft, syrupy kind. Toasting the flour is an important step and should not be skipped, as it greatly affects the taste. This is perfect served with tea.

9 oz dates, pitted
5 oz all-purpose flour
³/₄ c vegetable oil

serves 4

Check that there are no pits left in the dates, then mash them with a fork until soft.

Toast the flour in a large saucepan over medium heat (it will toast more evenly if you use a large pan). Stir regularly until the flour is golden brown and smells woody. This can take up to 15 minutes.

Pour in the oil and stir well until you have a brown paste, then add the dates and combine well. Keep over the heat for a few more minutes, until the mixture is perfectly fused and the bottom of the pan is clean (that's the test!).

Remove from the heat and with a spoon spread out on to a plate. Best served warm. I like to pour cream over it, too.

You can use a little bit of oil to reheat the afoosa when it hardens.

khabees

ARABIAN CRUMBLE

KHABEES REMINDS me of a Greek halva – later, I came to learn of its Ottoman roots. It is flour-based, as are so many desserts in the Gulf, but in contrast to the Mediterranean version this recipe calls for toasting the flour, which gives the dish a special depth and smokiness.

pinch of saffron strands

3 tbsp rosewater

4 oz sugar

3/4 c water

1/2 tsp cardamom powder

9 oz all-purpose flour, toasted

3/4 c melted unsalted butter or vegetable oil

serves 4

Soak the saffron in the rosewater for about 1 hour.

Bring the sugar and water to a boil in a medium pan. When the sugar has dissolved, remove the pan from the heat and stir in the cardamom powder and saffron water.

Toast the flour as in the afoosa recipe (see page 91). Stir the melted butter into the warm flour. The flour will first form clumps. Gradually add the sugared water (it will splatter, so be careful), stirring continuously, until the water is absorbed into a thick paste. Continue to stir over the heat for another minute or so until the bottom of the pan is completely clean.

Khabees is delicious with tea or on its own, and you will find yourself breaking off bits of it until there is none left.

balaleet
SWEET VERMICELLI

EVERYBODY LOVES BALALEET. This pleasing combination of sweet pasta and hearty omelette comes from the Indian subcontinent, where many versions are found. It's a difficult dish to pigeonhole. In the Gulf it may be eaten as a main course at dinner or served as a dessert. Shi'riya (vermicelli) is used throughout the Middle East to thicken soups and rice dishes.

pinch of saffron strands, plus
    extra (optional) for the
    omelettes
8 tbsp sugar
4 tbsp butter
1 lb 2 oz vermicelli
3 tbsp rosewater
4 eggs, beaten

serves 6

Dissolve the saffron in 4 tablespoons warm water and set aside.

Put 2 tablespoons sugar and 1 tablespoon of butter in a large pan of boiling water and cook the vermicelli for 3 minutes until al dente. Drain well in a colander. While the pasta is still in the colander, sprinkle with 5 tablespoons of sugar and toss well, preferably by shaking the colander, and without using any utensils, to dissolve the sugar evenly into the vermicelli.

Meanwhile, melt 2 tablespoons butter in a deep pan, taking care not to burn it, then sprinkle 1 tablespoon each of the sugar and the rosewater across the bottom of the pan. The sugar will quickly melt into the butter and start to caramelize. Do not stir. Immediately toss in the pasta.

Cut the remaining 1 tablespoon butter into cubes and place on top of the pasta. Pour over the saffron water and the remaining rosewater. Cover and steam over the lowest heat for about 40 minutes until the pasta absorbs the sugar and butter and the bottom caramelizes.

After about 15 minutes remove the lid – the butter will have melted. Pass a fork through the top layer of pasta without touching the bottom of the pan. The pasta will look set and drier on top and ready to be turned over onto a flat plate.

Fry the eggs in some oil or butter to make two thin omelettes. For extra flavor, add a few saffron strands when beating the eggs.

Turn the pasta out on to a large platter, top with the omelettes, and serve warm.

muhalbiyat al-sagoo
SAGO AND LYCHEE PUDDING

1 ADORE LYCHEES, with their luscious, translucent flesh and pretty pink shells. Sago is obtained from the trunks of various palms and is used across Asia as a thickener for soups and stews, and to make pudding. You can substitute other soft, sweet fruit like plums or pineapple but the sweet juice of the lychee blends very well with milk. This is an exotic take on the traditional sago pudding popular in Gulf cuisine, made with sago, sugar, and spices.

7 oz sago

3½ c reduced fat milk

3½ oz sugar

1 lb 4 oz can lychees

1 tbsp rosewater

serves 6

Wash the sago, then soak in cold water for 30 minutes (the grains will swell). Drain and set aside.

Heat the milk and sugar in a large, deep casserole, and whisk until the sugar has dissolved. Bring the mixture to a boil, then reduce the heat and add the strained sago, the lychee water from the can (reserve the fruit), and the rosewater.

Continue to stir the sago over low heat with a wooden spoon until you feel resistance. The sago will become translucent when it is cooked.

Reserve six whole lychees for the garnish and slice the remainder into quarters, then scatter them into six pudding bowls.

Pour over the sago and leave to cool completely before putting in the refrigerator. Garnish with whole lychees.

'igaili

CARDAMOM-SAFFRON SPONGE CAKE

THIS IS THE Arabian version of sponge cake, perfumed with the evocative scents of the East and traditionally accompanied by a cup of sweet black tea. It is the perfect cake: satisfying yet light, aromatic but subtle, enfolding a variety of seductive ingredients like sweet dates and sesame seeds, saffron and cardamom, and walnuts.

pinch of saffron strands

6 soft dates, pitted

5 eggs

5 oz sugar

1 heaping tsp ground cardamom

pinch of turmeric

4 oz all-purpose flour

2 tsp baking powder

1 tbsp vegetable oil

butter for greasing

sesame seeds for sprinkling

handful walnuts or other nuts
  of your choice, chopped

serves 6

Preheat the oven to 350°F (180°C). Soak the saffron in 2 tablespoons of warm water for about 1 hour, then set aside.

Mush the dates with a fork then roll small pieces into pea-sized balls. Set them aside.

Beat the eggs and sugar together for about 10 minutes, with a hand mixer or in a food processor, until light and fluffy. Add the cardamom and turmeric.

Sift the flour and baking powder into a bowl and, with a wooden spoon, fold 1 tablespoon at a time into the eggs. Continue folding as you pour in the saffron water and oil.

Grease a round 9-inch spring-release or ordinary cake pan with butter and line with wax paper. Dust the bottom and sides with a generous sprinkling of sesame seeds.

Pour half the cake mixture into the pan, scatter over the tiny date balls, then cover with the remaining mixture and a last sprinkling of sesame seeds. Top with the chopped walnuts.

Bake for 35 minutes until the cake is golden brown on top (a cocktail stick inserted in the middle should come out clean).

Cool the cake, then release the spring and turn out upside down on to a plate.

Serve with a spoonful of crème fraîche or a scoop of vanilla ice cream.

DATE-SYRUP DESSERT

ASEEDA MAKES AN appearance in winter and on special occasions. Much as pearl-divers traditionally used to cook rice in *dibs* (date-syrup) to fortify themselves, in the olden days new mothers were fed this dessert to help them regain strength after giving birth. Dibs can be sourced from any Middle Eastern grocer.

7 oz whole-wheat flour,
   pre-toasted
³/₄ c date-syrup (dibs)
⅔ cup melted unsalted butter
pinch of ground cardamom for
   sprinkling
hazelnuts, chopped

serves 6

Toast the flour as instructed in the recipe for afoosa (see page 91).

Bring the dibs and 4 cups water to a boil in a large pan. Place the toasted flour in a large pan and gradually combine with the dibs water, stirring continuously.

Put the mixture over the heat and bring to a boil. Stir in the melted butter and continue stirring until the pudding thickens and separates from the edge of the pan.

Pour into a long, flat platter and allow it to cool before placing in the refrigerator.

Spoon out into small bowls and sprinkle with cardamom and hazelnuts before serving.

salatat al-rumman wil jawafa
POMEGRANATE AND GUAVA FLOAT

THIS SUNNY RECIPE was made for my sister and me one dreary November afternoon by a dear friend. In this dish, the pomegranate's crunchy, ruby-red pearls swim in a sweet sea of guava and banana slices – the perfect antidote to the winter blues.

5–6 guavas, peeled and cubed

5 tbsp lemon juice

8 heaping tbsp sugar

2 large bananas, sliced

seeds of 2 pomegranates

serves 6

Put the guava cubes, lemon juice, sugar, and 4 cups iced water in a blender and process for about 2 minutes. The mixture should be neither soupy nor too chunky.

Pour into a large bowl and add the banana slices and pomegranate seeds.

Serve in small dessert bowls.

rangeena

STUFFED DATES IN BUTTER SAUCE

THIS IS ANOTHER Persian-inspired dish. Here, the dates are stuffed with walnuts (which I find a sublime pairing), but almonds could be used instead. I love desserts made with dates as there is no need for sugar.

1 lb 2 oz dates, pitted

3½ oz walnuts

7 oz butter

3½ oz all-purpose flour, toasted

serves 6

Preheat the oven to 325°F (170°C).

Break the walnuts into halves. Stuff each date with a walnut half and reconstruct the date (the shape doesn't need to be perfect) around the walnut. Place the stuffed dates upright, side by side, in a shallow dish.

Melt the butter in a saucepan, then combine with the flour and mix well. Pour the mixture over the dates, covering them.

Bake for about 15 minutes, just long enough for the dates to soak in the mixture and the top to harden.

Serve warm.

shraiba

CRUMBLY COOKIES

As a child, the golden crumbliness of these sweet cookies evoked the Arabian seashore and its sand. I still love them, and whenever we visit Kuwait, my aunt prepares a large batch for us. When I started making them, I was afraid the dough would crumble between my fingers, but that's the point, and once you get used to the texture, the rest is easy. *Nikhi* flour is made from chickpeas and is used in Indian cuisine to make flatbread.

7 oz whole-wheat flour

3½ oz all-purpose flour

3½ oz nikhi (chickpea) flour

5 oz confectioners' sugar, plus extra for dusting

1 c vegetable oil or melted unsalted butter

makes 30 cookies

Preheat the oven to 325°F (170°C).

Sift the flours into a large bowl, then mix in the sugar and vegetable oil. Using your hands, knead the flour until moist and crumbly, yet firm.

Divide the dough into small portions, then press between both palms and shape into rounds (the dough is likely to crack on the sides, which is normal, so do this with a light touch). Finally, press down your index finger very gently on the top to make a slight indentation.

Lay out on a baking sheet and bake for 15 minutes until lightly golden.

Dust with confectioners' sugar and eat and eat and eat!

gaimat

CRUNCHY DOUGH BALLS

O F ALL THE sweet recipes in this book, this is the most decadent. These seductive, syrupy dough balls torment the observant during the month of fasting, Ramadhan, when gaimat are a daily temptation. They are especially popular at *ghabqas*, snacktime events held in the late evening between *iftar*, the first break-fast meal, and *souhour*, the last nibble before fasting resumes at sunrise. *Shira* is the sweet dipping syrup.

1 lb 2 oz all-purpose flour

1½ tsp instant yeast

1 tsp ground cardamom

pinch of saffron strands

2 tbsp vegetable oil, plus
   2 c for frying

2 tbsp plain yogurt

FOR THE SHIRA

1 lb 2 oz sugar

pinch of saffron strands

2 cardamom pods

2 lemon wedges

serves 8

In a bowl mix the flour, yeast, ground cardamom, saffron, 2 tablespoons oil, and yogurt. Add 1¾ cups water and, with clockwise strokes, mix the dough by hand for about 10 minutes, until well blended. Cover and leave to stand in a dry place for at least 1 hour 30 minutes, until risen.

Combine the shira ingredients in a large pan with 2 cups water. Bring to a boil, then cook over medium heat until reduced and syrupy. A spoon dipped into the shira should feel sticky to the touch. Set aside.

If you are making this in winter, you may need to warm the dough slightly before frying it, either by placing it in a , very low oven or somewhere warm for a few minutes; otherwise, proceed directly to frying.

Heat the remaining vegetable oil in a large saucepan. With a teaspoon, take thumb-sized lumps of dough and drop them into the hot oil (make sure it's hot). While the dough cooks, reduce the heat to medium. Do this in batches. Fry the balls for about 10–12 minutes until golden. With a slotted spoon continuously turn the balls over so that they cook and brown all over. Place the balls in a colander and immediately dip them in the syrup. Turn them over once or twice, then strain them into a deep bowl.

Serve warm as they will be at their crunchiest.

tea and coffee

MILK TEA

Chai haleeb is a staple in the khaleeji home. It is a rich, sweet drink, enjoyed mornings and evenings with bread or a snack. Before the appearance of jams and croissants at the table, breakfasts (and often dinners) consisted of chai haleeb with flatbread.

Bring 4 cups water and 3 cups milk to a boil. Add good-quality black tea leaves, 4 cardamom pods, and 7 teaspoons sugar. Stir over medium heat until the sugar has dissolved, then bring to a boil. Simmer for 10–15 minutes. A milky skin usually appears, which you can either enjoy or discard.

chai lumi

LIME TEA

This is very popular during long Ramadhan evenings and is an excellent digestive.

Use 6 dried limes (lumi) per 4 cups water. Wash the limes, then remove the seeds and roughly chop. In a kettle, bring the lime pieces and 4 cups water to a boil for about 5 minutes, then simmer over the lowest heat for up to 30 minutes. Strain and sweeten to taste.

chai na'na'

MINT TEA

Mint is considered beneficial to one's health, which is why it is used in abundance in Middle Eastern cooking. At home, we have mint tea every day after lunch: it is a great natural digestive.

Boil 4 cups water. Put a heaping handful of washed mint leaves into a teapot, then add the boiling water. Allow to infuse for about 5 minutes.

chai za'faran

SAFFRON TEA

I love saffron in any incarnation, solid or liquid. This tea is amber-colored and very delicately flavored. *Ma' al-liqah*, date essence water, is used – it adds a subtle perfume.

Dissolve 7 teaspoons sugar in 4 cups boiling water. Add 1 teaspoon saffron and allow the mixture to infuse for about 20 minutes before adding 1 cup date-essence water (available in specialty shops). Infuse for 10 minutes then pour into *istikanas* (teacups), or small coffee cups. This can also be served cold: refrigerate the mixture for a few hours and serve chilled.

ARABIAN COFFEE

Coffee, *gahwa*, is the quintessential Arabian hospitality beverage, a welcome drink at gatherings in the majlis or diwan. Khaleeji coffee is amber-colored and scented with cardamom and saffron. It is poured from a large brass *dallah* – a gleaming coffee pot with a long, curved spout – into small enamel cups. In lieu of sugar, dates are offered. There is a ritual to coffee drinking. The pourer, al-maghawi, holds the dallah in his left hand, pouring out long streams of coffee into a stacked tower of cups held in his right hand. The drinker takes the cup in his right hand, never the left. Only a small amount of liquid – about a third of the cup – is poured each time and top-offs continue until the guest signals for the pouring to stop (a few tiny shakes of the cup from side to side).

In the dallah mix together 2 cardamom pods, 2 cloves, 1/2 teaspoon saffron (about 2 pinches), 1 teaspoon ground cardamom, and 1 tablespoon rosewater. Bring 3 cups water and 2 teaspoons roasted ground coffee to a boil over medium heat and cook for about 1 minute. Carefully and gradually pour the coffee liquid, not the residue, into the dallah. Allow to infuse for 10 minutes or so before pouring out. Do not shake, as that stirs up the coffee grains.

Pour into coffee cups and serve with dates.

glossary of terms

Daqous a fiery, salsa-like tomato sauce served with rice and meat dishes (see page 32).

Dibs date syrup, used as a substitute for sugar in cooking and baking. This recipe is from Iraq: Simmer 1 cup pitted dates and 1 cup water for 15 minutes. Add 1 teaspoon vanilla extract and simmer 5 minutes more. Add ½ teaspoon cinnamon, and process in a blender.

Diwaniyya or majlis especially popular in Kuwait, the diwaniyya is a private space (sometimes an external room in a house) where male family members, friends, and acquaintances gather, sometimes nightly, often weekly, to socialize or conduct business. Food and beverages are always served.

Furqa' crispy fried onion slices, sprinkled on top of rice. They add a caramelized, crunchy sweetness (see page 21).

Hakouka the crispy rice crust which forms at the bottom of the pan. It is a much-coveted delicacy.

Hashou a key ingredient in machbous dishes, the hashou is an aromatic, flavorsome mix that is either used as stuffing or to suffuse rice dishes.

Jareesh coarse, cracked wheat used for savoury porridge-like dishes. Also known as wheatberries. Bulgar can be used as a substitute.

Khubz rqaq wafer bread.

Lumi dried limes, also known as lumi Omani because of their provenance. They add a citrussy sourness to soups and stews. In the Gulf the darker variety is used for cooking. Lime powder is also widely used to spice chicken and fish stews.

Ma' al-liqah date essence water, used to perfume black tea and water.

Machbous (plural: michabees) epitomizes khaleeji cuisine. Michabees are biryani-like dishes made with meat, fish, or vegetables (truffle machbous is a fine delicacy). Machbous meat is cooked in the same water that is used to cook the rice, and all the ingredients suffuse together during steaming.

Mashkhoul aromatic white rice, also called 'aish (Arabic for living).

index

acknowledgments

Many people have helped with the making of this book:

In the UK: Clare Sayer and Rosemary Wilkinson at New Holland Publishers; Antonio Leanza at the London School of Photography; Sue Atkinson, Sunil Vijayakar, Belinda Altenroxel and Roisin Nield for a magical photo shoot; Roger Hammond at Blue Gum Design for putting the words and pictures together so beautifully; Mitch Albert, Wasan al-Saleh and so many of my friends, who took turns as editors and food-tasters; and my cooking buddy Asmahan Siti-Taher.

In Kuwait and Bahrain: Saribudeen Abdulrahman, Ibrahim Abul and family, Nasra 'um Abdullah' Afifi, Babu Damodara-Nallani, Hamad Darwish, Nuha A. al-Ghanim and family, Mohammed Hussain Ismail, Salwa and Nada Kanoo, Hamza Kutty, Paula Mansour, 'um abdulrazzaq' and Khalid al-Mishaal, Noufal Moodadi, Khokon Peris, Faten al-Qaseer, Ali Riponullah, Fitaliss Rosario, Tony Santan-Fernandes, Shamali Sweets Factory, Qasim Sultan, Mark Williams and Uwe Wruck. With special thanks to Ali al-Saleh and his wonderful family, Wajeeha, Betool and Khatoun al-Saleh, and to the one-and-only Afaf al-Mosawi.

Most of all: my aunt, the formidable Hessa al-Hamad, for offering up her kitchen, cooks and recipes over the course of a year, for putting up with the intrusion of cameras, laptops and photographers, and for dishing out quantities of sustenance throughout; my friends Monica Meehan – for encouraging me to take the idea of this book seriously, and for testing the fish recipes – and Jana Gough, who went in search of dried limes and rosewater one Easter weekend, and for her impeccable editing; and Razan al-Saleh, practically this book's co-author, for her boundless generosity in sharing so much of herself, her family and friends. And always, heartfelt thanks for their support to Laila and Ahmed al-Hamad.